CULTIVATING THE ENERGY OF LIFE

CULTIVATING THE ENERGY OF LIFE

BY LIU HUA-YANG

Translated and introduced by
Eva Wong

SHAMBHALA
Boston & London
1998

SHAMBHALA PUBLICATIONS, INC.
Horticultural Hall
300 Massachusetts Avenue
Boston, Massachusetts 02115
www.shambhala.com

© 1998 by Eva Wong

⊗ This edition is printed on acid-free paper that meets
the American National Standards Institute Z39.48 Standard.

Distributed in the United States by Random House, Inc.,
and in Canada by Random House of Canada Ltd

Library of Congress Cataloging-in-Publication Data
Liu, Hua-yang, d18th/19th cent.
  [Hui ming ching. English]
  Cultivating the energy of life/Liu Hua-yang; translated
    and introduced by Eva Wong.
      p. cm.
  ISBN 1-57062-342-2 (pbk.: alk. paper)
  1. Hygiene, Taoist. 2. Exercise therapy—China.
  3. Taoism—China. I. Wong, Eva, 1951- . II. Title.
  RA781.L545 1998   97-24079
  613—dc21   CIP

BVG 01

CONTENTS

INTRODUCTION   *3*

Historical and Philosophical Background   *7*

Teachings of the *Hui-ming ching*   *17*

TREATISE ON CULTIVATING LIFE
Hui-ming ching

1 The Dissipation of Life Energy   *23*

2 The Six Phases of the Circulation of Fire   *29*

3 The Jen (Function) and
Tu (Governor) Meridians   *33*

4 The Fetus of the Tao   *37*

5 Emergence of the Fetus   *41*

6 The Transformations of the Body   *45*

7 Facing the Wall   *49*

8 Absolute Extinction in the Void   *53*

CONTENTS

DISCOURSE ON THE CORRECT
METHOD OF CULTIVATION
Cheng-tao hsiu-lien chih-lun 57

DISCOURSE ON THE CORRECT
METHOD OF ENERGY WORK
Cheng-tao kung-fu chih-lun 71

DISCOURSE ON STILLNESS (CH'AN)
AND MOVEMENT (CHI)
Ch'an-chi lun 91

THE NINE STEPS
OF REFINING THE MIND
Chiu-tseng lien-hsin 103

CULTIVATING THE ENERGY OF LIFE

 INTRODUCTION

To live a healthy and long life, to be tranquil and untouched by the dust of the mundane world, and to become one with the life-giving energy of the Tao—these are the goals of the practitioner of Taoist spirituality. Health, longevity, and inner peace are highly valued in Chinese culture, and throughout the history of China, the Taoist arts of health were practiced by hermits, householders, scholars, administrators, and businesspeople. Today, in Hong Kong and Taiwan, herbal foods, meditation, ch'i-kung exercises, and internal martial arts are popular subjects on television talk shows, and even a casual visitor to a Chinese bookstore will not fail to notice that the most popular books are the ones on health and longevity.

As interest in the Taoist arts of health grows in the West, the demand for books on meditation and ch'i-kung (the art of circulating internal energy) has increased. As a practitioner of the Taoist arts, I believe the best way to present the literature of the Taoist spiritual tradition is to let the sages speak for themselves. While a book *about* a subject can be a useful introduction, secondary sources cannot replace the immediacy of listening to the teachers themselves. For the non-Chinese reader, translations are therefore still the best way to approach the literature of Taoism. However, written knowledge is not intended to replace oral teachings, and to acquire practical knowledge, one must seek the guidance of a teacher.

The *Hui-ming ching* is probably the most important Taoist treatise on the arts of longevity written in recent times. When it was first published in 1794, the Taoist community was both shocked and delighted. Departing from tradition, the *Hui-ming ching* abandoned the symbolic language typically used in the ancient classics and discussed the Microcosmic and Macrocosmic Orbits, the role of breath in circulating energy, and the conservation of procreative energy in a straightforward and concrete way. It is also one of the few Taoist treatises that describe the landmarks of spiritual development and document the process of spiritual transformation from start to finish. Even two hundred years after its publication, the *Hui-ming ching* is still one of the most accessible works on a branch of Taoist practice that has been shrouded in mystery for hundreds of years.

The word *hui* in the *Hui-ming ching* means wisdom. It refers to the wisdom-mind that directly intuits the Tao. *Ming* means life. It refers to the primordial energy of the Tao that gives life and form to the body. Together, *hui-ming* means uniting wisdom-mind (or original nature) with the energy of life, an apt title for a classic on cultivating body and mind.

This book contains a complete translation of the *Hui-ming ching* and its major commentaries. The original texts are published in the *Wu-liu hsien-tsung* (Techniques of Immortality by Wu and Liu), which is a collection of the writings of Taoist masters Wu Chung-hsiu and Liu Hua-yang.

The *Hui-ming ching* was first introduced to the Western public by Richard Wilhelm in a German translation. It was published with the *T'ai-i chin-hua tsung-chih* (The Treatise of the Golden Flower) under the title *The Secret of the Golden Flower*. Unfortunately, Wilhelm's translation (and the English version of Cary F. Baynes) was based on an incomplete text of the *Hui-ming ching*: the commentaries and the most important sections—the illustrations—were missing. Moreover, the Wilhelm-Baynes translation is severely biased by Jungian psychology and does not present the book from the Taoist spiritual perspective. Not only are the historical and philosophical connections with its major influences—the Complete Reality school of Taoism, Ch'an (Zen), and Hua-yen Buddhism—ignored, but the teachings of the Wu-liu sect, which form the spiritual foundation of the *Hui-ming ching*, are not acknowledged.

We cannot appreciate the spiritual value of a text if we superimpose a particular perspective on it, especially one that comes from a different culture. To understand the spiritual meaning of a text, we need to yield to the text and let it speak on its own terms. Yielding to a text is not simply suspending judgment. Yielding requires us to throw ourselves into the world of the text and be embraced by its meaning.

To enter the meaning-world of the text, we must become acquainted with its historical and philosophical background and understand the perspective of the authors. However, once the perspective of the authors is understood, we need to free the text from its historical and philosophical context and listen to it as if it were a trusted teacher. When the text develops a personal meaning for us, it will begin to speak as a spiritual advisor. Finally, we need to let go of our personal attachment to the text, so that the text can take us beyond our personal experiences and become a guide to the frontiers of spiritual consciousness.

 HISTORICAL AND PHILOSOPHICAL BACKGROUND

The Wu-liu Sect

The Complete Reality school of Taoism founded by Wang Ch'ung-yang was one of the most influential Taoist sects that emerged in the Sung dynasty (960–1279 C.E.). Advocating the dual cultivation of body and mind, it synthesized the internal alchemical arts of longevity, the meditation techniques of Ch'an (Zen) Buddhism, and the ethics of Confucianism. After the death of Wang Ch'ung-yang, the Complete Reality school was split into a northern branch led by Ch'iu Ch'ang-ch'un, who was one of the Seven Taoist Masters, and a southern branch led by the famous internal alchemist Chang Po-tuan. The main difference between the two branches of the Complete Reality school lies in their approach to the cultivation of body and mind. First, the northern

7

branch taught that mind should be cultivated before body, while the southern branch advocated that body should be cultivated before mind. Second, the northern school of Ch'iu Ch'ang-ch'un disapproved of the use of sexual yoga to gather internal energy, while the southern school of Chang Po-tuan did not. Finally, the initiates of the northern branch took monastic vows of celibacy, while the practitioners of the southern branch were primarily laypeople. Given these differences, it is not surprising that the northern school attracted young practitioners, while Chang Po-tuan's sect appealed to older people.

Throughout the Yüan (1271–1368 C.E.) and early Ming (1368–1644 C.E.) dynasties, the teachings of the northern and southern branches of the Complete Reality school continued to diverge. The northern branch, especially the Lung-men sect, incorporated ceremony and monastic discipline into their practice, while the southern branch relied more and more on sexual techniques to cultivate internal energy. By the late Ming, the change in spiritual priorities within the Lung-men sect was beginning to cause discontent and disillusionment among some of its members. One of them was a high-ranking initiate named Wu Chung-hsiu, who felt that blind devotion and harsh discipline were not conducive to spiritual training. Wu tried to reform the sect from within but was unsuccessful. In 1615 he left the Lung-men sect and wrote the *Huo-hou ching* (Treatise on the Phases of Applying Fire). In this treatise, Wu laid out a program of spiritual training that combined the methods of stilling the mind and the techniques of conserving and circulating internal energy. Wu Chung-hsiu's synthesis of what he called the "best" of the northern and southern forms of Complete Reality Taoism found a large following among people who wished to learn the arts of longevity but were not interested in the orthodoxy and devotional practices of the Lung-men sect.

In the middle of the Ch'ing dynasty (1644–1911 C.E.), the teachings of Wu Chung-hsiu were developed further by Liu Hua-yang, who integrated Wu's form of Complete Reality Taoism with Ch'an and Hua-yen Buddhism. Like Chang Po-tuan, Liu Hua-yang practiced Ch'an Buddhism before he began his training in the Taoist arts, and like Chang, he did not embrace Taoism until he was past middle age. Liu brought together what he thought was the best of Buddhism and Taoism by synthesizing the internal alchemy of conserving and circulating internal energy, the Ch'an method of meditation, the visual imagery of Hua-yen Buddhism, and the idea of spirit travel from Shang-ch'ing Taoism. His unique approach to the cultivation of body and mind is presented in a series of treatises that include the *Hui-ming ching*, the *Cheng-tao hsiu-lien chih-lun* (Discourse on the Correct Method of Cultivation), the *Cheng-tao kung-fu chih-lun* (Discourse on the Correct Method of Energy Work), *Ch'an-chi lun* (Discourse on Stillness [ch'an] and Movement [chi]), and the *Chiu-tseng lien-hsin* (The Nine Steps of Refining the Mind). These texts and the commentaries written by Liu's students are the culmination of Liu Hua-yang's lifetime of experience in practicing and teaching the Taoist arts of health and longevity.

The Influence of the Complete Reality School and Taoist Internal Alchemy

The influence of the Complete Reality school is evident throughout the *Hui-ming ching*. The Wu-liu sect's techniques of cultivating the body are similar to those of the southern branch, and its methods of stilling the mind resemble those of the northern branch of Complete Reality Taoism. Therefore, it is not incorrect to say that the Wu-liu sect took the "specialties" of the northern and southern branches of the Complete Reality school and integrated them into a new system of knowledge.

The southern Complete Reality school focused on cultivating the body and recovering internal energy. Its techniques were originally designed to help people who started their training in the internal al-chemical arts late in life. For Chang Po-tuan and Liu Hua-yang, the leakage of generative or procreative energy at and after puberty was the major cause of the loss of the energy of life. Consequently, both masters emphasized the gathering, cultivating, and refining of ching (generative or procreative energy). There is one difference, however, between the teach-ings of Chang Po-tuan and those of Liu Hua-yang. While Chang would utilize techniques of sexual alchemy to gather generative energy from a partner, the Wu-liu sect did not use such methods. Both Wu Chung-hsiu and Liu Hua-yang believed that genera-tive energy can be gathered, cultivated, and refined within the body of the practitioner without the help of a sexual partner.

In the *Hui-ming ching*, the key to cultivating the body lies in circulating the energy of life in the Mi-crocosmic and Macrocosmic Orbits. Once the leak-age of generative energy is curbed, life energy can be gathered, transformed, and circulated within the body. The flow and the ebb of internal energy are regulated by applying the correct amounts of heat during specific phases in the cycle of circulation. The heat required for refining the energy is gener-ated in the lower tan-t'ien (energy field), and the cir-culation of the energy in the Orbits is controlled by the breath. Thus the fast breath, called the warrior fire, is used to push energy through the body, and the slow, quiet breath, called the scholar fire, is used to steam and incubate the stored energy. In this respect, the Wu-liu method of cultivating energy is similar to the internal alchemical techniques described in the *Tsan-tung-chi* (Triplex Unity) and the *Lung-fu ching* (Dragon-Tiger Classic). The Wu-liu practitioners and the traditional Taoist alchemists both believed that the key to health and longevity lies in transforming the mundane body into a subtle body, where energy is conserved and regenerated constantly.

After the generative energy is refined, it is transformed into vapor and stored as a bundle of energy in the lower tan-t'ien (a field of energy located near the navel). Called the true seed, this bundle of energy is a spiritual fetus (yüan-shen) that needs to be protected and nurtured. At this stage of spiritual development, the meditation methods of the northern branch of the Complete Reality school are used to still the mind and to facilitate the incubation of the spirit-fetus.

During the incubation period of the spirit-fetus, the practitioner may experience lights, colors, and sounds and see images of deities, enlightened beings, and landscapes of the immortal realms. These sensations are landmarks of spiritual progress and will only appear when the practitioner has reached a certain level of development. Visual imagery is not a part of the spiritual experience of Complete Reality Taoism, and to understand the images and sensations described in the *Hui-ming ching*, we need to look at the influence of Hua-yen Buddhism on the teachings of Liu Hua-yang.

The Influence of Buddhism

The influences of Ch'an and Hua-yen Buddhism are seen throughout the *Hui-ming ching*. In the illustrations, the meditation posture shown is the full-lotus posture of Ch'an, and the practitioner is depicted as a Buddhist with a shaved head and not a Taoist with a topknot. The Taoist ideas of the Microcosmic Orbit, the spiritual fetus, and the Golden Elixir are blended with the Buddhist notions of returning to original nature and being liberated from reincarnation. Because of the strong Buddhist influence in its teachings, the Wu-liu sect is often called the school of Hsien-fo ho-tsung (the Combined Path of the Immortals and the Buddhas).

The *Hui-ming ching* adopted the Ch'an idea that there is no separation between wisdom (Skt. *prajna*; Chin. *hui*) and stillness (Skt. *samadhi*). Also, like Ch'an Buddhism, it believed that meditation is a tool to cultivate wisdom and that it is possible to attain enlightenment in this body during this lifetime. However, for Liu Hua-yang, attaining stillness is a means and not an end. This is where the Wu-liu sect departs from Ch'an Buddhism. In Wu-liu practice, meditation is used to gather and circulate internal energy as well as to recover original mind.

There are many references to the *Hua-yen ching* throughout the *Hui-ming ching*. The *Hua-yen ching* is the Chinese name for the *Avatamsaka-sutra*, which is commonly known in English as the *Flower Ornament Scripture*. Although the *Hua-yen ching* was translated from Sanskrit into Chinese in the fifth century C.E., it remained obscure until a school of Buddhist thought named Hua-yen was formed by the monk Fa-tsang in the seventh century. From then on, the *Hua-yen ching* became one of the most important Buddhist scriptures in China.

A central idea of Hua-yen Buddhism is that existence is divided into the Realm of Principle and the Realm of Facts. The Principle is static, unchanging, and formless. It is the void. The Facts are dynamic and changing, and have specific manifestations that are identifiable as forms. This is the phenomenal world. The two realms interact with each other and exist in an interdependent harmony. These teachings of Hua-yen Buddhism are consistent with the Taoist understanding of the Tao as simultaneously the underlying permanent reality and the changing flux of things in transformation. However, it is not this philosophical worldview but the rich visual imagery of the *Hua-yen ching* that had the most impact on Liu Hua-yang's teachings.

The influence of Hua-yen imagery is most prominent in the *Hui-ming ching*'s discussion of the conception of the spiritual fetus and its birth. When life energy has been refined and transformed into vapor, it will collect in the lower tan-t'ien as a bundle of energy. This bundle of energy is called the spiritual fetus or the Child of the Buddha. When the fetus materializes in the lower tan-t'ien, rays of light will emanate from the body of the practitioner. These images are similar to the *Hua-yen ching*'s description of the light radiating from the hair and between the eyebrows of the Buddha when he attained enlightenment. As the spiritual fetus matures, the body and mind continue to be transformed. The Taoist practitioner begins to acquire occult powers, and like the enlightened Sudhana entering the abode of the Manjushri Buddha described in the *Hua-yen ching*, he is transfigured mystically. When the spiritual fetus is born, it first appears as a single entity, but with time, it can be manifested as multiple bodies. This is similar to the *Hua-yen ching*'s notion of "a body extending everywhere." When the fetus of the spirit first emerges from the body, it hovers above the head of the practitioner and does not wander far. However, as the spirit matures, it will travel farther and farther to different realms to learn from the immortals and enlightened beings.

Spirit Travel and the Influence of Shang-ch'ing Taoism

Spirit travel was first practiced by the shamans of ancient China. It was said that the legendary emperors Yao, Shun, and Yü all journeyed to the celestial realm to learn from the deities. Taoists as early as the fifth century B.C.E. also practiced spirit travel. Descriptions of the spirit leaving the body to travel to other realms of existence are found in both the *Chuang-tzu* and the *Lieh-tzu*. One group of Taoists, however, made spirit travel the center of their practice and developed it to a level of sophistication unmatched in any other sect. They were the Shang-ch'ing Taoists, and although their influence is not explicitly acknowledged by Liu Hua-yang, their teachings are evident in the *Hui-ming ching*'s description of the maturation and education of the spirit-child.

Shang-ch'ing Taoism was founded by Lady Wei Hua-ts'un in the third century during the Chin dynasty (265–420 C.E.). The goal of the Shang-ch'ing

Taoist is to enter into an ecstatic union with the Tao. This union is accomplished by visualizing the deities who are the manifestations of the Tao and by journeying to their abodes in the sun, moon, and stars. Shang-ch'ing celestial travel consists of two stages—leaving the earth to fly to a celestial body and wandering from one constellation to another. The former is a short sojourn away from the earthly realm, while the latter is a long journey that takes the spirit of the practitioner to the far reaches of the celestial realm. These two stages of Shang-ch'ing celestial travel parallel the two stages of spirit travel in Wu-liu practice. When the spirit-child first emerges from the body, it too makes only short journeys away from the body. However, as the spirit-child matures, it will go farther and farther from the body of the practitioner, wandering from one realm of existence to another to learn from the immortals and enlightened beings. Finally, when the spirit has learned how to return to the Tao, the Wu-liu practitioner voluntarily sheds the body-shell to allow the spirit to return to the primordial energy that originally gave it life.

 ## Teachings of the *Hui-ming ching*

The teachings of the *Hui-ming ching* are concrete and straightforward. They can be summarized as follows:

1. When we were in our mother's womb, we were filled with the primordial energy of the Tao. In the natal state, original nature and the energy of life are united.

2. At birth we come into contact with the world. When air is inhaled through the nostrils, the primordial breath within is contaminated and the connection with the Tao is broken. Original nature and life energy separate, the former moving to the heart and the latter moving to the kidneys.

3. At puberty, sexual desire is aroused. When the primordial life force is transformed into procreative energy, it begins to leak out of the body. The leakage of life energy is the primary cause of aging, illness, and premature death.

4. If the leakage is stopped and the procreative energy is drawn back into the body, the energy will be transformed into the primordial vapor of the Tao. When there are no openings for the vapor of life to escape, it will circulate through the Microcosmic Orbit in the body. In the *Hui-ming ching*, this circuit is called the Dharmic Wheel.

5. With time, enough vapor will gather to form a bundle of energy in the lower tan-t'ien. This bundle of energy is the spirit-fetus.

6. The spirit-fetus is nourished by the primordial

vapor until it is mature. This process is called the incubation of the fetus.

7. When the spirit-fetus is ready to be born, it will exit the body at the top of the head. Manifesting as multiple entities, the spirit becomes omniscient and the practitioner can see the past and the future.

8. Initially, the spirit-child hovers around the head of the practitioner. But as it matures, it will travel farther and farther from the shell that conceived it. In its journey to the different realms of existence, it will learn how to return to the Tao.

9. Finally, when the spirit has completed its training, the practitioner willingly gives up the shell to liberate the spirit for its final return to the Tao.

As a spiritual text, the *Hui-ming ching* offers profound insights on the meaning of health, longevity, and immortality. The Wu-liu masters believed that the goal of cultivating body and mind is to prepare for death as well as to prolong life. Thus, the *Hui-ming ching* is a book on how to live and how to die. Unlike Taoist alchemy of the third through the tenth centuries, Wu-liu Taoism does not try to escape death or believe that immortality can be attained in the physical body. Accepting that the physical body has a life span, the Wu-liu Taoists believed that the goal of life is to recover the primordial vapor of the Tao and liberate it at death. In this revolutionary re-definition of immortality, the Taoist arts of health and longevity are not so much a means to attain eternal life on earth or in other realms as a way to recover our connection with the Tao so that the spirit can return to its original home when our time in the earthly realm is over.

TREATISE ON CULTIVATING LIFE

Hui-ming ching

CHAPTER 1
*The Dissipation
of Life Energy*

THE SUBTLETIES OF THE Tao lie in original nature and life, and to cultivate original nature and life is to return to the One. The ancient sages used symbols when they spoke of returning original nature and life to the One because they did not want to present the teachings in a straightforward way. Consequently, nowadays it is difficult to find someone who truly understands the meaning of cultivating mind and body.

I have not broken the oath of secrecy by compiling the illustrations and presenting them in this book. I have only taken the teachings of *Hua-yen Scripture* and the Taoist classics and described them as pictures.

The key to cultivating life lies in the One cavity.

The illustrations are intended to help fellow spiritual seekers to understand the meaning of the dual cultivation of mind and body so that they will not stray into erroneous paths. The pictures show how the true seed is conceived within the body, how the energy of life is lost, how the Child of the Buddha is cultivated, and how the Tao is attained.

FIGURE 1.
Hui-ming ching Illustration 1: Picture of Leakage.

Each illustration in the *Hui-ming ching* is accompanied by phrases that are mnemonics of instruction (k'ou-chüeh). The phrases are written in a Chinese literary form in which two phrases form a pair. The pairs are arranged side by side. Thus, the upper two phrases form one pair and the lower two phrases form another pair. Since Chinese is read from right to left, the phrase on the right is always the first half of the pair.

The four seven-word phrases read: "If you want to stop the leakage and attain the indestructible golden body, focus on the radiance and do not leave the happy grounds. Practice diligently to temper the root of life. Always keep the true self hidden in its home." The circle in the abdominal area of the figure is the cavity called the Gate of Life (ming-men). The path that leads from the cavity to the outside is called the path of leakage.

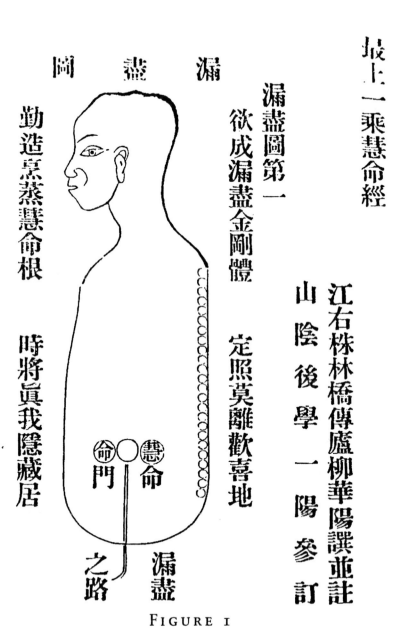

最上一乘慧命經

漏盡圖第一

欲成漏盡金剛體　定照莫離歡喜地

漏盡圖

勤造烹蒸慧命根　時將真我隱藏居

山陰　後學　一陽　參訂

江右株林橋傳廬柳華陽譔並註

慧命

命門

漏盡

之路

FIGURE I

The One cavity is the root of the void. It has neither shape nor form. When the original vapor emerges, the cavity appears; when circulation is at rest, the cavity disappears. The One cavity is the place where the sacred is hidden. It is the altar of life, and it has many names—the Palace of the Dragon at the Bottom of the Sea, the Land of the Snowy Mountain, the Western Realm, the Original Gate, the Land of Great Happiness, and the Home of the Limitless. If the practitioner of the arts of longevity does not understand this cavity, he or she will wander through thousands of lifetimes not knowing where to look.

This cavity is great and wonderful. It emerged when we were conceived in our mother's womb. In it, original nature and life are intertwined like flames in a furnace and are united with the Laws of the Celestial Way and the Great Harmony. Therefore it is said that before birth and creation, inhalation and exhalation are limitless.

Before we were born, we were a fetus, a round shape inside our mother's womb. When the womb is filled with the primordial vapor, the shape inside stirs, the shell breaks, and like a mountain crashing down, the fetus tumbles out. In the infant's first cry, original nature and life are separated. From then on, original nature does not recognize life and life does not communicate with original nature. Thus we go from infancy to youth and from youth to old age and death.

The Tathagata Buddha in his compassion has revealed a method that will help people to return to the womb. By uniting original nature, life, spirit, and vapor and returning them to the One cavity, our true essence can be recovered. It is as if the original vapor of our parents has reentered this cavity to create a fetus.

Inside the One cavity is the Ruling Fire. At the gate guarding it is the Subordinate Fire. Throughout the body is the Common Fire. When the Ruling Fire stirs, the Subordinate Fire will burn and support it. When the Subordinate Fire moves, the Common Fire will follow accordingly. In the way of mortals, the three fires follow the forward path; in the way of the Tao, the three fires follow the reverse path. Therefore, the One cavity that dissipates the energy of life is also the cavity where the sacred form emerges. You will receive no benefits if you take the incorrect paths. If you try tens of thousands of methods looking for the One cavity outside and do not understand that the key to life lies within, you will waste time and effort and accomplish nothing.

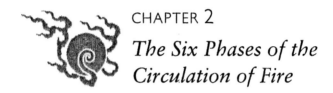

CHAPTER 2

The Six Phases of the Circulation of Fire

THE TAO IS A WHEEL that is always turning. Like a cart rolling down a road, it does not wait for the lazy and tardy. The schedule of applying fire and heat must be accurate and the procedure must be followed in detail. The method is described in figure 2. When the process of firing is complete, the true image will come from the west. This is the key to everything. The secret lies in inhalation and exhalation. The coming and going of the breath are like opening and closing a circuit. The true intention must rise and fall in the internal world. This movement is likened to letting go of oneself and yielding to others.

In no way does this illustration leak the secrets of the Celestial Way. The foolish and ignorant will not understand it because the Celestial Way does not reveal the Tao to individuals who are not virtuous. The relation of virtue to the Tao is like the relation of a bird to its feathers: one cannot exist without the other. You must be dedicated, filial, upright, honorable, and pure and must observe the five abstinences before something will happen. All the secrets you need to know are found in the *Hui-ming ching*. Study it carefully and you will attain the ultimate reality.

FIGURE 2.
Hui-ming ching Illustration 2: Picture of the Six Segments of the Dharmic Wheel.

Two sets of phrases accompany this picture. The first set consists of four seven-word phrases that read: "The Patriarch of Buddhism has opened up the road to return to the beginning, revealing the city of happiness in the western realm. Turn the Dharmic Wheel constantly to lift yourself to the celestial realm. Make the breath subtle in inhalation and exhalation to return it to the earth."

The four five-word phrases read: "Timing is divided into six segments. In one instance you will return to the origin. The Tao emerges from it. You need not look for methods outside."

There are six segments on the ascending part of the wheel (the right half) and six on the descending part (the left half). At the top of the wheel is the sky; at the bottom is earth. These points represent the transition between the ascending and descending segments. Ascent is inhalation and descent is exhalation. The processes of purification and cleansing occur at the mid-points of the ascending and descending pathway of the Dharmic Wheel.

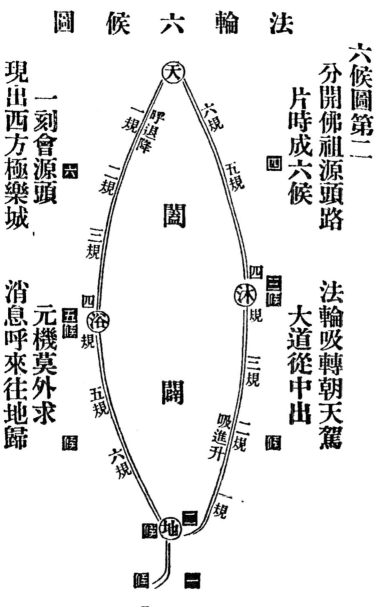

法輪六候圖

六候圖第二

分開佛祖源頭路
片時成六候

法輪吸轉朝天駕
大道從中出

現出西方極樂城

一刻會源頭

元機莫外求

消息呼來往地歸

天

六規
五規
四
三規
沐
四規
三規
二規
吸進升
一規
地
二

一規
呼退降
二規
三規
四規
浴
五規
六規

闔
闢

FIGURE 2

CHAPTER 3

*The Jen (Function)
and Tu (Governor)
Meridians*

INSIDE THE BODY IS A
pathway called the Dharmic Wheel. The goal of figure 3 is to describe it to fellow practitioners. If the
two meridians are open, the hundred other channels
in the body will also be open. The deer sleeps with
its nose against the anal orifice to complete the circuit of the tu meridian, and the crane and the tor-
toise connect the circuit of the jen meridian naturally. If these animals can live a thousand years,
there is no reason why humans cannot. If those who
cultivate the Tao can turn the Dharmic Wheel, they
will be able to circulate the energy of life, attain
longevity, and realize the Tao.

FIGURE 3.
Hui-ming ching Illustration 3: Picture of the Two
Meridians.

The four seven-word phrases read: "The Original Gate and
the path of subtle breath are revealed. When all thoughts
cease, the Dharmic Wheel will circulate in the hundred
channels. Always tend and stoke the fires in the cavity of
longevity. Pay attention to the bright pearl and the gate that
transcends death." Liu Hua-yang goes on to say that this
picture is the same as the previous one (fig. 2) and that he is
describing identical processes of transformation in slightly
different terms so that readers will not miss his message.

任督二脈圖

咽　喉

督脈　　任脈

任督二脈圖第三

現出元關消息路　常教火養長生窟

蓋此圖於前二圖原是一也。所重續者何爲是恐修道之人不知

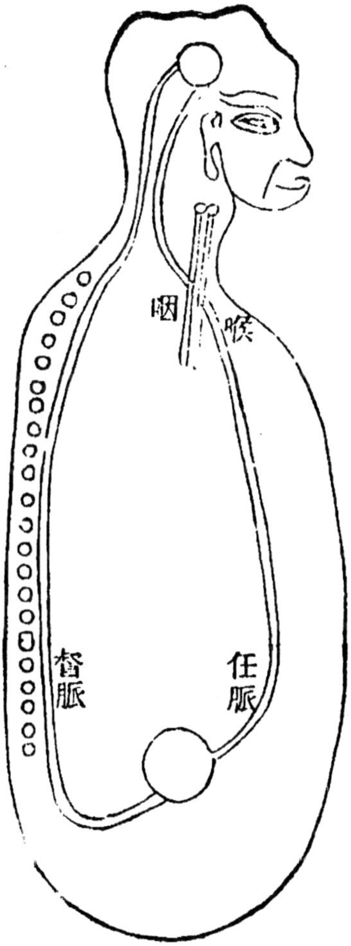

休忘百脈法輪行　檢點明珠不死關

FIGURE 3

CHAPTER 4

The Fetus
of the Tao

THIS PICTURE (fig. 4) is based on the teachings of
the *Hua-yen Scripture.* The ordinary monks did not
understand the meaning of the fetus of the Tao because the teachings were not described to them. In
this book I shall explain the teachings so that everyone will know that the Tathagata Buddha knew
about the sacred fetus of the Tao. This fetus has neither shape nor form. It is created from two substances and is produced by the spiritual vapor
within. First the spirit enters the vapor, then the vapor embraces the spirit. When spirit and vapor are
united and intention is still, the fetus will emerge.
When the vapor coagulates, the spirit will become
numinous. The scripture describes the two sub-

stances as "coming close and responding to each other." Nourishing one another, the two will grow and mature. When vapor is sufficient, the fetus will become round. Eventually it will emerge from the head. This phenomenon is called the fetus emerging when the form is complete. The fetus of the Tao is also called the Child of the Buddha.

FIGURE 4.
Hui-ming ching Illustration 4: Picture of the Fetus of the Tao.

The two seven-word phrases read: "Apply the method without effort and diligently let the radiance penetrate. Forget the form and take care of the internals to help the true spirit grow."

The two five-word phrases read: "Incubate the fetus with fire for ten months. Bathe and cleanse it in warmth for a year."

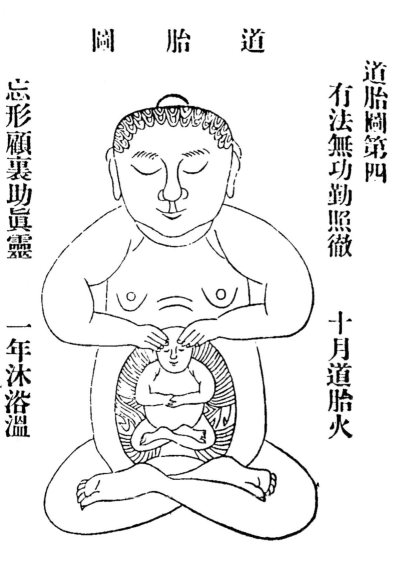

道 胎 圖

道胎圖第四
有法無功勤照徹
十月道胎火

忘形顧裏助眞靈
一年沐浴溫

FIGURE 4

CHAPTER 5

*Emergence of
the Fetus*

THE HUA-YEN SCRIPTURE
says, "A hundred rays of light came forth from the
top of the Lord Buddha's head and a thousand-
petaled lotus emerged from the light. On the lotus is
the Tathagata Buddha. Ten rays of a hundred sacred
lights are seen radiating from his head and spread-
ing to all directions. Everyone who saw it welcomed
the light-emanating Tathagata." The spirit described
in the scripture is the emerging yang-spirit. It is also
called the Child of the Buddha. However, if you only
recite the teachings of Ch'an (Zen) and do not know
the method of cultivating life, you will not be able to
maintain your body and realize the Taoist Child of
the Lord Buddha. In revealing the secrets of the

Hua-yen Scripture, I have made its teachings available to future generations. In this way, everyone can attain the Tao, build the sacred internal environment, and be liberated from the dust of the world.

FIGURE 5.
Hui-ming ching Illustration 5: Picture of the Fetus Emerging.

The four phrases read: "The body beyond the body is called the face of the Buddha. The spirit-mind without the mind is the Bodhi. The thousand petals of the lotus are emanations of the vapor. A hundred rays of light will shine on the image when the spirit is gathered."

出胎圖

出胎圖第五
身外有身名佛相

千葉蓮花由㷊化

念靈無念即菩提

百光景耀假神凝

FIGURE 5

CHAPTER 6

The Transformations of the Body

FIGURES 6A AND B.
Hui-ming ching Illustration 6: Picture of the Body
Becoming Many Bodies.

A "As mind divides and shape emerges, the true form rises
from the cavity. Together with the spirit, it is transformed into the void."

B "When there is nothing coming in or going out, the wonderful Tao is realized. The form divides into spirit-bod-
ies to return to the true origin."

化身圖第六

分念成形窺色相

共靈顯迹化虛無

FIGURES 6A AND 6B

CHAPTER 7

Facing the Wall

FIGURE 7.
Hui-ming ching Illustration 7: Picture of Facing the Wall.

The four phrases read: "The spirit fire is transformed into an empty form. The light of the original nature radiates within to return to its true origin. The mind's seal hangs high in the sky like the shadow of the pure moon. The raft reaches the shore in the glow of the light of the sun."

面壁圖

神火化形空色相　心印懸空月影淨

面壁圖第七

性光返照復元真　筏舟到岸日光融

FIGURE 7

CHAPTER 8

*Absolute Extinction
in the Void*

FIGURE 8.
Hui-ming ching Illustration 8: Picture of the Void
and Dissolution.

The four seven-word phrases on the right and left of the
circle read: "One bright ray of light hovers over the dharma
universe. When both are forgotten, stillness is numinous
and empty. In the void of the great expanse, the celestial
mind shines. The waters of the ocean are clear and the
moon is reflected in the deep lake."

The pair of four-word phrases above the circle read:
"When there is no birth, there will be no death. Nothing
leaves and nothing comes."

The pair of seven-word phrases below the circle read:
"When the clouds scatter, the sky is blue and the mountain-
scapes are clear. Returning to life in ch'an stillness, the full
moon stands alone."

虛空粉碎圖

粉碎圖第八

一片光輝周法界　虛空朗徹天心耀

不生不滅

無去無來

雙忘寂淨最靈虛

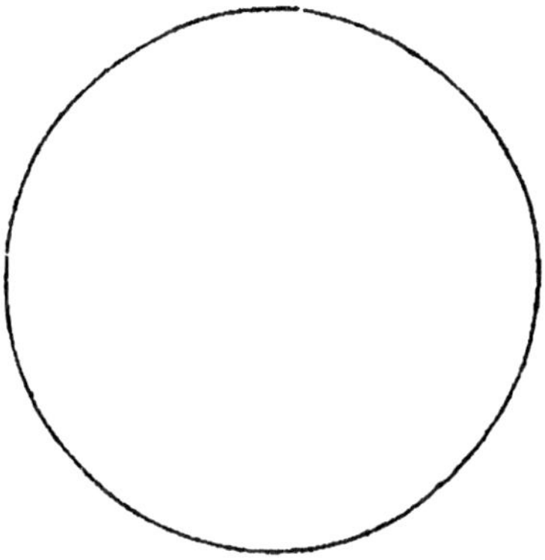

雲散碧空山色淨

慧歸禪定月輪孤

海水澄清潭月溶

FIGURE 8

DISCOURSE ON THE CORRECT METHOD OF CULTIVATION

Cheng-tao hsiu-lien chih-lun

LIU HUA-YANG SAID:

In cultivating life, one must restore lost energy. In refining life, one must use fire to transform the substance. Fire must be accompanied by wind before it can be effective. Moreover, there must be a place for the vapor to be collected and stored. The intelligent ones of both past and present all used the method of wind and fire to cultivate original nature and life. It is a pity that nowadays many are uninformed and only a few know the secret teachings. Most people cultivate original nature but neglect to preserve life. Because they do not understand the principles of movement and stillness, all their efforts have come to nothing.

When the energy of life is stirred, it flows out of the body. When all the energy has dissipated, we die. If we die, where would original nature be? And how could the Tao live in us? This is why the enlightened ones observed the cycles of movement and stillness and cultivated themselves accordingly.

The root of life is in the kidneys. When the kidneys are active, water is produced. The root of original nature is in the heart. When the heart is active, fire is produced. If the fire is immersed in water, original nature and life will not dissipate.

Fan the fire with wind to produce the true seed. The method is straightforward, and those who understand it will cultivate the true seed and attain enlightenment. Wait when it is still; gather when it stirs. Put both substances (life and original nature) in the same furnace. This process is called transformation by fire. Walk the path taken by the Tathagata Buddha and sit under the Great Teacher's tree. The movement of fire follows the sequence of the transformations. If monsters appear, you should strengthen yourself with the warrior fire and prevent the life energy from rushing out of the body. Hold on to clarity and stillness. Preserve harmony within. Bathe frequently in the vapor to strengthen and protect the foundation of the pearl. Circulate it by turning the Dharmic Wheel, calling on the warrior and scholar fires alternately. Whether or not you will grasp the subtleties will depend on the instructions of your teacher and your intuition.

When the seed of enlightenment is mature, the warrior fire should be stopped and the scholar fire should be used to incubate and gather the vapor of life. To incubate means to preserve. When a bright pearl appears, all the monsters will be dissolved. Gently circulate the pearl through the path of the Great Channel. When the fetus of the Tao is completely formed, your intelligence will increase a thousandfold. Incubate it so that your life is anchored in the Tathagata. When life energy does not stir, you should cultivate stillness diligently. As the glow of the numinous spirit increases, let it shine to illuminate your intuition. Do not sink into boredom, drowsiness, or confusion. The strength of your stillness will depend on the emptiness of original nature and the one true intention. When the dharma self is still, snowflakes will be seen fluttering around. This state is called "coming out of stillness." For when the Tao has reached the height of stillness, it will move again. The wheel starts to turn at the time of tzu (11:00 P.M. TO 1:00 A.M.). The movement of the true substance must be anchored in stillness: this is the key to rebuilding the wondrous way and reestablishing life. When stillness is anchored, the limits of the limitless are reached.

COMMENTARY

At birth we were endowed with original nature and life. When the vapor of life reaches its height at puberty, it begins to leak out of the body. If we can get guidance from a teacher before the leakage occurs, there will be no need to recover lost energy, and we can enter the realm of the Tathagata immediately. On the other hand, those who have lost life energy must replenish it so that the body can be whole and healthy. They must use movement and stillness to direct the vapor of life inward and gather that which was lost. When life energy is not excited or stirred by desire, we will become immortal.

The substance transformed is none other than the primordial vapor within. The primordial vapor is secluded inside its cavity. When stirred, it flows out of the body as mundane energy and is lost. If the energy is returned to its original place, it will be transformed into vapor by fire. The transformation, however, will not occur if you apply only wind. Wind and fire must be used together. Inhalation and exhalation must work in synchrony to fan the fire and transform the energy into vapor. The intention must be directed to the vapor's cavity and the breath must be used to reverse the flow. It is important that these two functions be performed together.

In hundreds and thousands of generations, the enlightened ones who pursued the Tao with diligence all used the method of wind and fire to cultivate original nature and life. Today many people try to practice the teachings of the Buddha by reciting the scriptures; some try to live their lives according to the precepts; and the most advanced adepts practice ch'an [stillness] meditation. However, only a few understand the meaning of original nature and life. Many claim that the Buddha taught only the cultivation of original nature. They do not know that original nature and life are emphasized equally in the great teachings of the Mahayana. If you do not understand the function of movement, your meditation will be unproductive. Practicing the incorrect method will not only hinder progress but also cause you to regress, so that all your efforts will come to nothing.

There are many who claim to be the followers of the Buddha but have not received the true teachings of the Tathagata. They are attached to their own conceptions of original nature and do not understand the importance of cultivating life. Thus, when the energy of life stirs, they do not know how to gather it. Although the life force does not leak out, it is not cultivated, and if the life energy is not cultivated, it will be wasted. When the resources of life are gone, death will come. When death comes, how can you attain the Tao?

The ordinary person thinks that he or she can cultivate the Tao by leaving the family to live in the remote mountains and valleys or in a monastic community. They think that by sitting in stillness they can attain the Tao. They do not know that without the true teachings, they will not understand the meaning and function of movement. As a result, their quietude is like living death. They are like the cat who guards an empty hole, waiting for the mouse to appear.

If you do not know the function of movement, you will waste your time, and all your efforts will be in vain. If you want to cultivate life, you must still your mind and wait for movement to occur in the kidneys. Once movement is experienced, you should begin to refine the heart and the kidneys. When the heart and kidneys are united, original nature and life will become one. This is what the ancient sages meant by "uniting the pair."

Life energy is primordial vapor. When vapor stirs, it becomes water. Original nature is the true intention. When intention moves, it becomes fire. The heart's intention must be directed to be united with the vapor of the kidneys. When the vapor is attracted to intention, it will not flow outside. Wind is breath and fire is intention. Although the leakage is curbed when vapor is attracted by intention, there may be remnants of untransformed life energy left in the body. These residues can stir up desire and create problems. Mencius called it the breath that distracts intention. The *Hua-yen Scripture* calls it the monster in the shadows. These shadowy monsters can be transformed into bright light only through discipline and determination. When the monsters are dissolved, the heart and the body will be peaceful and feelings of desire will not arise. This is what the World Honored One [Buddha] meant when he said that "we must enter the three fires to conquer the fire dragon." These are the secret teachings of both Buddhism and Taoism. If you follow these methods, your desires will disappear naturally and the mind will be still. This is what is meant by "using the Tao to tame the mind and using the mind to connect with the Tao." With practice, the celestial movement will be initiated in the body. Substance will emerge from nonsubstance, and the true seed will appear.

The difficulty in cultivating the Tao lies in the existence of many incorrect methods. If people have the good karma to encounter this method, the rest of the training is simple and straightforward. Even if you start at eighty years of age, you could attain the Tao in your lifetime. However, if you do not receive the true transmission, you will not be able to intuit the teachings no matter how hard you try. Many Ch'an Buddhists only teach people how to empty their minds and sit in stillness. The method that I am expounding, however, will teach you how to gather the true seed, refine it, and transform it into the Child of the Buddha. The key to this method is, before movement occurs, you must abide in stillness and wait for the movement to happen; when movement occurs, you should use intention to hold it. The World Honored One called the unification of intention and vapor the transformation by fire. The path of the movement of fire through the jen and tu meridians is called the Dharmic Wheel. The Bodhi tree is the pure land of the tan-t'ien. The World Honored One entered this realm when he attained perfect stillness under the Bodhi tree.

Master Tao-i once said, "If there is no movement, there is no stillness; if there is no stillness, there is no movement." When life energy moves, intention moves. When life energy is still, intention is still. The shadowy monsters in the body are the dark vapors of untransformed energy. Appearing as hallucinations or dreams, these vapors can block bodily functions and cause illness. In meditation they appear as monsters, and in dreams they appear as wild animals. The dark vapors are dangerous because they can dissipate life energy and harm the seed of the Buddha. If you sense their presence, you must increase wind and fire to refine and temper yourself. Burn the monsters with fire, drive away the shadowy ghosts with wind, and you will not meet with danger. When the monsters no longer appear, use intention to incubate and care for the seed. Initiate the movement of the Dharmic Wheel. Use the warrior fire to control the rise and fall of energy and use the scholar fire to bathe and purify it. The flow and the ebb of fire also have their warrior and scholar components. Although your teacher may reveal the secrets of these functions to you, you will need to use your intuition to grasp the subtleties.

When the seed of the Buddha is conceived, use the scholar fire to embrace it. If you use the warrior fire instead, the seed of the Buddha will be dispersed. This is a critical time in your training and you should be extremely careful. When the seed of the Buddha is conceived, stop the breath of the warrior fire and use the scholar fire to draw the sacred light inward. Simultaneously, use the true intention to nourish it and protect it from danger. When the proper foundations are built, the seed of the Buddha is ready to be born. The seed is the bright pearl. When it is mature, it will have a definite shape and form. When the bright pearl emerges, the hundred monsters are driven away. This process is called absolute extinction.

The seed of the Buddha is strengthened as it moves through the spinal column. If the momentum is slowed, the seed will not develop properly. When the seed enters the Central Palace, white hair will become dark, fallen teeth will grow again, and intelligence and intuition will be enhanced. You will know the past and the future, and your wisdom will be limitless. At this time, if you use the scholar fire to steam and bathe the seed, nothing can go wrong. Once you have understood the procedures, the knowledge will always be with you. When stillness settles in the Central Palace, wisdom will shine on the ocean of original nature. *Ch'an* means stillness, and *Thatness* means original nature. When you reach this stage of development, you will need only to cultivate the stillness of original nature and regulate the fire of your breath. There is no need to engage the wisdom of knowing. With time, the original nature in the womb of the Tao will become increasingly numinous. Knowledge of the past and future, fortune and misfortune, should not affect your practice. In absolute stillness, let the inner light glow. True knowing and true seeing must take hold before the true form of original nature can be realized. This is what the *Hua-yen Scripture* means by "clearing the mind and extinguishing the consciousness of knowing." If stillness is stagnant, there will be no breath in the fetus and you will be trapped in unproductive meditation. If stray thoughts arise, the fetus will wander off, the fire will cool, the vapor will dissipate, and nothing will be accomplished. Whether stillness can be maintained in the womb will depend on the state of mind. In the ten months of incubating the fetus, the intention must be focused on the womb. When thoughts cease and the breath is still, the fetus will mature. The *Hua-yen Scripture* says, "When absolute stillness takes hold, ch'an will anchor knowing." This is what is meant by "not entering the path of death."

If you see snow or flowers fluttering around while you are meditating, you will know that the fetus is mature. At this time, images of the emerging fetus will begin to appear. It is important that you allow the fetus to come out. If you keep it in the womb, the spirit will not become numinous. Thus, although the fetus is mature, it will not accomplish anything.

The substance of pure yang begins to move once perfect stillness is attained. Pure yang cannot be exhausted. The enlightened ones patterned themselves after the sun and moon and deduced the principles of the cycles of change. The sages kept this method secret because they were afraid they might reveal the Celestial Way to those who are not ready.

In practicing the method of cultivating and refining life energy, you must gather the precious substance inside. You must guide the entity conceived within and unite it with the energy of life. With time, you will be able to enter and stay in the great stillness.

DISCOURSE ON THE CORRECT METHOD OF ENERGY WORK

Cheng-tao kung-fu chih-lun

LIU HUA-YANG SAID:

When you first learn to cultivate life, you should practice your meditation in a quiet room. The body should be like a tree and the mind should be like cold ashes. Let the light of the spirit be your guide. Put original nature and life in the same place. This is the first step in cultivating the Tao.

When stillness has reached its height, movement will begin. This movement is the root and leaf of the Tao, the creator of all things. When energy swirls in the One cavity, draw it in and do not let the life force flow outside. Hold on to it, let it grow, and then harmonize and dissolve it within. In this way, the foundation of the fetus of the true seed will be strong. These are the teachings of the True Way.

What the ancients described as "transformation by fire," "unity and harmony," "the Bushel"—all refer to the workings of the Tao. When you have reached a certain level of cultivation, a substance will emerge from nothingness. At this time, you must direct it to flow backward instead of forward.

Bodhidharma called this the process of gathering. When the substance has returned to its origin, the Dharmic Wheel will turn. Opening and closing, ascending and descending, it will establish itself in the celestial mind. Following the jen and tu meridians, the substance will return to the roots and renew your life. This is what the four cycles and the six phases are about.

There are specific methods for gathering and directing the precious substance through the gates. If you only gather and do not create, or create and do not gather, you do not have the right method. If you want to learn the correct way, you must ask a teacher to help you. You must also cultivate the strength of the Dharma Body before you can attain the Tao.

The rise and fall of the fire in the furnace is controlled by intention. When intention is still, the precious substance will be born. This is what the Tathagata Buddha meant by "lighting the fires of the furnace." If you see the image of the Shakyamuni Buddha before you, do not be afraid. When movement begins, you must be careful. Do not allow the substance to leak outside. After the movement has penetrated the mouth of the Ganga river, it will climb to the top of Mount Sumeru. When it enters the Flower Realm of the Southern Splendor, you will find yourself seated in the sacred hall of the Buddha of Light. Suddenly flurries of snow, falling like spring rain, will swirl around in the Central Palace. This is a sign that you have conceived the fetus of the Tao. Now you must sit in peace, contentment, and stillness. Cultivate the fetus by not thinking about it. Help it to grow by incubating it in stillness and bathing it in light. When stillness is absolute, you will suddenly see a bright moon suspended in the sky. Hold on to the round moon and wait. Soon a shaft of light from the red sun will rise toward the center of the moon. At this time you should gather the light and hide it within. When all is still, you should practice the method of dissolution by returning both the substance and nonsubstance to the undifferentiated chaos. This is called wu-wei.

The Great Tao is limitless. When stillness has reached its height, movement will begin. When the one substance is united with the fetus of the Tao, the Dharmic Wheel will turn. After the movement has run its course, all is still again. When this stillness is extinguished in the void, the fetus will be mature and filled with energy. A thousand petals will flutter around, and the Child of the Buddha will emerge in stillness to rise beyond the three realms. This is the emergence of the Tathagata Buddha.

When the fetus first emerges from stillness, it must be watched carefully so that it will not be attacked by monsters. The wheel of the golden light is the spirit within. If it is gathered and returned to the origin, it will be transformed into the wonderful medicine. Cultivating it is like creating and nourishing children and grandchildren.

Finally, you should make the necessary preparations to hide in a deep valley far from the dust of the world, and return to the void to be united with the Tao. This is the Tathagata Buddha's final task. I hope that those who share my aspirations will not be distracted by the so-called teachings of Ch'an and regard the true way as false.

COMMENTARY

The meditation room should be located in a place where you will not be disturbed. When you meditate, you must let go of form. Attain stillness but do not attend to the mind. Draw the light inward and let original nature enter the palace of life. In this way, original nature and life will be cultivated simultaneously.

When true stillness takes hold, movement will begin. This is not conscious intention or activity in the mind but the movement of vapor in the tan-t'ien.

The Fifth Patriarch [Ch'an master Hung-jen] described it as the "emergence of feeling," and the Sixth Patriarch [Ch'an master Hui-neng] spoke of "the desirous mind" as "the Tao mind." If students do not understand the nuances of this teaching, they will not know the meaning of movement. As a result, they will not know where to begin and how to progress.

The World Honored One knew how to use movement to build the tan-t'ien and cultivate the Child of the Buddha. Thus he was able to transcend the ordinary and enter the sacred. Do not underestimate these teachings, for they are the foundations of cultivating the Tao.

The ordinary person does not know the method of cultivating and refining life. Thus, when movement occurs, the mind is stirred and the life force flows out uncontrolled. Mencius spoke of this as "emotion arousing the intention." Following the path of mortals, men and women use the energy of life to procreate, just as males and females of all life-forms use their energy to copulate and create the ten thousand things. However, while other life-forms only expend energy to procreate, humans use the energy for pleasure. Moreover, the ordinary person believes that the enlightened ones too desire sexual pleasure. They misunderstand the teachings because they do not know that the Buddha had waited in stillness for the movement of the life force to stir and had used fire to refine it and wind to fan it before the mind was excited. When the external kidneys [the testes] are drawn in and the mind is like clear water, how can there be sexual desire? When the seed is directed inward by the wind, how can there be desire in the mind? These things are part of the natural way of the Tao and are the forces that move the sky and the earth. Everything must happen naturally. The mind must not be engaged. This is the key to transforming the ordinary into the sacred. Everything hinges on the secret of the clockwise and counterclockwise movement.

The ancient sages had several names for the primordial vapor. They called it substance, water, and that which is produced in the chamber. The ailimportant cavity is the cavity of the vapor located in the tan-t'ien. When it is open, it is the Life Gate. The medical treatises identify it as the area between the kidneys. For both men and women, this is where the procreative energy flows out. The words *wisdom* and *life* were used by the World Honored One to describe what the Chinese had traditionally called the primordial vapor. When we were conceived in our mother's womb, we were endowed with this vapor, which is the force that created all things. Our Buddha nature is also contained in this vapor because the vapor is also the celestial mind and original nature. It flows through the eight meridians and is connected to the mother's breath. Therefore the fetus does not breathe through its nose or mouth when it is in the mother's womb. When it emerges from the womb, however, the shell is broken, and its mouth and nose come into contact with the world. But because the eight meridians are still sealed, the primordial vapor remains locked within. At puberty the primordial vapor surges through the gates and flows out. Once the vapor begins to dissipate, the cavity can no longer be closed. From here on, when movement occurs, the vapor will drain out of the body.

There was a disciple of this school named Yüanming, who lived in the Golden Mountain, received his training there, and became the abbot of the Wing-shui monastery. Of the Ch'an teachers, he said, "They do not talk about the leakage of energy. They are only concerned with cultivating the mind." Since these teachers also suffer from the leakage of energy, they are no different from the ordinary person. The *Hua-yen Scripture* says, "If there is desire in the body and the mind, the roots of desire are not severed." People heat cinnabar and hope that it will become rice. After hundreds and thousands of years, they are still left with cinnabar grains. Without the correct method of training, they wander through countless reincarnations and are unable to attain liberation. It is hard to believe that many teachers of Ch'an do not talk about the life energy. The teachings of the World Honored One on wisdom and life were transmitted to generations of Bodhisattvas. If these teachings are followed, the three desires will be extinguished.

Breathing consists of inhalation and exhalation. However, if intention is not present, the breath in the tan-t'ien cannot be regulated. The correct method of breathing involves steaming and incubating. When the life energy has returned to the place of its origin, the breath will be soft and intangible. At this time the true intention must be used to guard the energy. Treat it like sparks in the furnace. When intention and vapor are united, they will be transformed into the true seed. Out of nothingness, a substance will emerge. This is how life energy and original mind are cultivated simultaneously. If you stray from this path, your efforts will come to nothing.

Fire is the true intention. Once original nature and life are united, you should draw the gaze inward to the tan-t'ien. Situate the true intention in the position of the northern waters in the body. It was said that when the Third Patriarch of Ch'an Buddhism sat in the middle of the stream and entered the state of absolute extinction, his students asked him to teach them. After being asked three times, he finally transmitted the true method of the hidden eye to them.

You cannot complete the cultivation of original nature and life in a day or a night. Years of hard work and discipline are required before you will succeed. The time needed to complete the training will depend on when you begin your practice and whether you are diligent or lazy. Progress is not measured by hours and minutes but by the time it takes for the precious substance to emerge. When the substance is born, the mind will recognize it intuitively. If you sit in stillness and do nothing, you will lose the opportunity to gather it. When the substance appears, it has a tendency to drain out of the body. If you let it flow in a clockwise direction, it will run out, but if you reverse the flow, it will be directed back into the body.

Life energy originates in the tan-t'ien. From there it flows up the back and down the front of the body. This circuit is called the Dharmic Wheel. The movement of the life energy is driven by both internal and external breathing. When the external breath descends, the internal breath rises; when the external breath rises, the internal breath descends. Moving in synchrony with the breath, the energy first swirls to the top of the head and then drops into the abdomen. This is what the Sixth Patriarch [Hui-neng] meant when he said, "I have a substance. Upward, it supports the sky. Downward, it sinks into the earth."

The celestial mind is the Yellow Center. It is situated between the sky and the earth and is called the Celestial Pivot or the Handle of the Bushel. In the macrocosm of the sky, it is the celestial mind. In the microcosm of the body, it is the true intention in the Central Palace. If you lose the true intention, your body will be like a minister without a sovereign. The true intention is the cog that anchors the turning of the wheel. It must be present in the Central Palace when the Dharmic Wheel is set in motion. When the Dharmic Wheel turns, intention and life energy must move together in the tu meridian. If intention moves but life energy does not, or vice versa, the Child of the Buddha will not be conceived.

If you want to return to the original ground, you must contain and gather the vapor. Let the energy rise and fall. Steam it and incubate it. When you have understood this method and practiced it, the cavity of life will gradually be filled with vapor. If you can maintain your stillness, the celestial movement will begin. When the vapor circulates through the body, the yang substance will be full and numinous and you will feel happy and harmonious. When the substance becomes numinous, it should be gathered and circulated. Let it flow through the three gates and direct it into the Central Palace. This method has been kept secret for a long time because no one has dared to talk about it.

If you gather the vapor at the inappropriate time, the substance will lose its freshness. If you do not catch it when it first stirs, you will lose the opportunity to collect it. These problems can occur if you do not obtain instructions from a teacher. Many students of Buddhism do not receive the complete teachings. Thinking that they know everything, they belittle their teacher and are lazy in their practice. As a result, they have no knowledge of the secret teachings. However, if you are humble and sincere and are willing to respect and preserve the dharma, the teachers will transmit the instructional mnemonics to you. Virtue is the structure of the Tao, and original mind is its function. If you follow a teacher but do not cultivate virtue, the teachings will not take hold. Virtue is related to the Tao as feathers are related to a bird. If either is missing, nothing will be accomplished. Knowledge of the method, hard work, and charitable deeds are all required for the true intuition to take hold. There are many people who, while claiming to cultivate the Tao, are attached to power, fame, recognition, and wealth. Do not be deceived by them. You must acquire the Buddha Body before you can master the way of the Buddha. The enlightened ones have known this all along, but many students still believe that they can attain the Tao simply by sitting still. They only know that Master Liu attained the Tao by sitting in silence, but they do not know that his merits matched those of the Sixth Patriarch.

The furnace is in the tan-t'ien and the intention must be directed to it. The Tathagata said, "If you do not know where the mind and the eyes are located, you cannot conquer the dust and sweep away the troubles." Whether or not the substance will emerge from the furnace will depend on the strength of the true intention. The substance is the primordial vapor. The Tathagata of the Purple Light tells us that when the fire is warm and movement is initiated, the Child of the Buddha will be conceived. Internally, you will experience sensations of warmth; externally, you will see images. These images can make you anxious if you do not understand the true teachings. When images appear, do not be afraid. Maintain stillness regardless of what you see. If the mind is stirred or if the spirit is dulled, the seed of the Buddha will dissipate.

The spinal column is sometimes called the

Ganga river or the Ts'ao stream. If its course is blocked, you must direct the true intention to clear the river mouth and open the pathway that leads to the top of the head. The top of the head is called Mount Sumeru. The throat is called the many-story pagoda because it is divided into twelve segments. Wisdom emerges when the circuit is connected to the origin. It is said that when the Discourse on the Dharmic Law was first expounded, the Dragon Lady presented a pearl to the south, transformed herself into a man, and attained Buddhahood. The south symbolizes the cavity of the mind. In its mundane state, the mind prefers movement to stillness. It wants to be excited by new things; it shifts and stirs; it enters and leaves the cavity casually; and it does not know how to return to its original home. From birth to death and through the various forms of life in the six realms of existence, it wanders about without direction and purpose. Death comes because we do not understand the nature of mind. However, if we know how to use wisdom and life to tame the wayward mind, we can change our animal nature into original nature and transform the knowledge-spirit into the original spirit. The process is likened to using lead to confine quicksilver. When quicksilver is coupled with lead, it becomes inert and loses its wayward nature. Therefore you must direct original nature and life into the mind's cavity before they can be tamed. Otherwise, no matter how diligent you are in your practice, you will be stuck with the knowledge-spirit of post-creation and never attain the original nature of pre-creation. Original nature entered life when we tumbled out of our mother's womb. Thus original nature is also called celestial destiny. Those who practice the way of the Buddha should understand the difference between pre- and post-creation. If you are ignorant in these matters, nothing will be accomplished.

The cavity of the Sacred (Central) Palace is located below the heart. It is where the fetus of the Tao is nourished. When the Child of the Buddha enters this place, the body will feel like floating clouds and falling rain. The hundred channels will be open and circulation will flow to the four limbs. When this happens, you must immediately rotate the mind's eye left and then right thirty-six times. Next, rotate it right and then left twenty-four times. Finally, you should let it settle in stillness. Original nature and life will now be gathered in the Central Palace to nurture the fetus of the Tao. Once you have reached this stage of development, you will never lose what you have attained. You will be in a state of bliss and happiness because you have now entered the true stillness of ch'an.

When the fetus of the Tao is first conceived, the post-creation breath is still tangible although elusive. This state is called forgetting the form. At this time you must direct your intention to the spiritual womb and maintain absolute stillness. Do not become sleepy or bored. Be alert and awake at all times. This state is called illuminating the form.

When you see the moon rise from the tan-t'ien, use the true intention to hold it. Unite the sun and moon, gather them, and hide them within. Remain in the absolute stillness of the void and let no thoughts arise. When everything has returned to the origin, the Great Tao will emerge. Movement will begin again when stillness has reached its limits. The pure yang substance will rise from the Bubbling Spring and enter the Central Palace to embrace the fetus of the Tao. After this substance has merged with the fetus of the Tao, it will descend to the lower tan-t'ien and flow to the base of the spine. From there it will rise to the top of the head and then drop into the Central Palace again. This precious substance is the source of nourishment for the fetus. When nostril breathing becomes faint and intangible, supreme stillness will take hold and the circulation in the six channels in the arms will be at rest. When you see flowers falling, you will know that the fetus is mature; if not, the fetus is still incomplete. When you see images of falling flowers, you should let the intention emerge from stillness. Direct it to leap out of the Central Palace; channel it to the crown of the head; and then guide it down to the Life Gate. These are the sensations that accompany the emergence of the Tathagata, and they are described by the *Hua-yen Scripture* as "rays of light emanating from the World Honored One."

When the spirit first leaves the body, images of Bodhisattvas may appear. If they talk to you, do not answer them and do not let your intention wander. Let the spirit leave and enter naturally but do not allow it to travel far. The emerging spirit should not be attached to the ten thousand myriad things. When a wheel of bright light appears, move your Dharma Body toward the light. Merge with it and draw it into the mundane body. Once the mundane body and the Dharma Body are united, feed it with the energy of life. Gradually the mundane body will be transformed into vapor. If the mundane body is not nourished by the golden light, impurities will settle, and the body will not be transformed into vapor. The amount of impurities collected will depend on the amount of virtue and merit you have accumulated. The secret teachings of the celestial wheel have now been completely revealed.

When the spirit first ventures out of the body, it is manifested as a single entity. With time, however, it will be manifested as countless bodies. Once you have accomplished the countless manifestations of the spirit, you should find a hiding place deep in the mountains where no one will disturb you. Sit in stillness and transform the body into vapor. Eventually the spirit will return to its formless state in the void.

DISCOURSE ON STILLNESS (CH'AN) AND MOVEMENT (CHI)

Ch'an-chi lun

LIU HUA-YANG SAID:

In the way of the Tao and the Buddha, original nature and life are symbolized by the dragon and the tiger. The dragon represents movement and the tiger represents stillness, and the cycle of movement and stillness is the key to the secret work in the body. The ancient Buddhas said that the great Tao cannot be attained without the knowledge of original nature and life. All the Buddhas and the patriarchs attained enlightenment by cultivating and refining original nature and life according to the principles of stillness and movement.

Original nature and life are united when we are in our mother's womb. At birth they are separated into distinct entities. Before puberty the precious life force is strong and plentiful. However, when the primordial substance of life is aroused by the physical and emotional changes that accompany puberty, it will leak out of the body. If we can prevent this leakage by turning the light inward and guiding it with intention, we can send the precious primordial substance back to the Northern Sea. This is the process of harmonizing, uniting, and gathering the substance. Because the substance can circulate in a clockwise or counterclockwise manner, the process is often referred to as the secret work. If it is not called the secret work, people will not understand the important role of the supreme treasure in the circulation of the energy of life.

If you sit in silence but do not understand the unity of original nature and life, you will be trapped in unproductive stillness and will never find the true seed. When movement stops, stillness is manifested as non-differentiation—this is called ch'an. At the height of stillness, movement will begin again—this is called chi. At this time you must hurry and gather that which is round and spinning about. Initiate the movements of opening and closing and set the primordial workings of the Dharmic Wheel in motion. In this way the true precious seed will return deep into the roots. The ancient sages called this the way of recovering life and returning to the origin.

Gather the seed of the Buddha by exchanging action for nonaction. Illuminate it in silence and stillness. Where the heart and the eyes meet is where you will find the pearl of Shakyamuni. The pearl shines like cinnabar and is shaped like a snowflake. It tastes like thick soup and is sweet like honey. Active and playful, it flows everywhere. You must not be anxious or suspicious when you are practicing the secret work. Wait patiently for the circulation to occur. This is a most wonderful and effective way of gathering the essence of life. When energy moves, it will penetrate the three iron gates. This is called transcending mortality and entering the sacred.

When the sacred pearl of Shakyamuni has returned to the center, you should hold on to it gently and let it glow—this is ch'an. In the stillness of ch'an, you will feel a deep sense of happiness and bliss. However, in the center of nonaction, suddenly there will be action—this is chi. If nonaction is not named chi (or movement), people will not know that such a wondrous thing exists and will only focus on the womb of the fetus. When the wonderful substance has run its course and is guided back to the womb to settle in prolonged stillness—this is ch'an, or the process of extinguishing birth and death. When stillness is absolute, a substance will suddenly appear—this is chi. Waiting for it to gather —this is ch'an. When it emerges—this is chi. Gather and hide it, letting it glow softly while holding on to it—this is ch'an. When it is illuminated in stillness, two substances will flow out of the Bubbling Spring cavity—this is chi. After gathering it, there is a period of stillness—this is ch'an, or the process of dissolution. When everything is dissolved, snowflakes will be seen fluttering around—this is chi. At this time, you should come out of stillness without delay. If you let the seed stay in the womb, the mysterious transformation will be lost. When the fetus emerges, it will be liberated from the three realms. Waiting in stillness for it to emerge completely—this is ch'an. When a shaft of golden light is suspended in space— this is chi. Gather and direct it inward, letting stillness settle in stillness—this is ch'an. After a long period of stillness, form and spirit will both dissolve. This is the end of the cycles of ch'an and chi. I hope that all those who practice the way of the Buddha will not be led astray by the devious ways of false teachers who speak about the method of ch'an but do not understand the secret work.

COMMENTARY

When we were born, we were endowed with original nature and life. To attain the Tao is to recover the original nature and life that were once a part of us. Original nature and life are symbolized by the dragon and the tiger, and the natures of the dragon and the tiger are manifested as movement and stillness. Movement is called chi and stillness is called ch'an. Many names have been used, but they all refer to original nature and life. Anything other than original nature and life are not real and are the products of the imagination of those gone astray. Many schools try to penetrate the secrets of original nature and life but fail to grasp the essentials. Some cultivate original nature; some cultivate life; but none of them know how to cultivate both. In the end, they all fail because they do not know that original nature and life must be cultivated simultaneously before we can attain the Tao.

The nature of mind is described as ch'an and the nature of the kidneys is described as chi. When we are conceived in our mother's womb, the vapors of our father and mother are joined. A point of numinous light, which is original nature, is enclosed in the fetus. This is what the ancients meant by "harmonizing the three families to produce the body." At birth we scream and tumble out of the mother's womb onto the ground. Original nature moves to the heart and life enters the kidneys. The two are separated by eight and four-tenths inches and for most people, original nature and life remain apart through old age to death.

At about fifteen or sixteen years of age, the primordial vapor of pre-creation hidden in the tan-t'ien begins to stir. When the way of post-creation directs the order of things, the vapor of pre-creation is excited. If this vapor is not cultivated when it first stirs, it will force open the gates of yang, be transformed into its post-creation form, and dissipate out of the body.

When chi [movement] occurs, images appear internally and the testes are stimulated externally. The patriarch Chi-wu [Absolute Emptiness] said, "Direct the spirit into the cavity and the vapor will return to its cavity naturally." The World Honored One said, "Where the heart is, there are the eyes." To unite the heart and the kidneys is to direct the heart to the kidneys. When the flow is clockwise, the vapor becomes procreative energy and will leak out of the body. When the flow is reversed, or counterclockwise, the vapor is transformed into the primordial vapor, which is the precious substance of life. Chi is movement. The primordial vapor is the life force. When the vapor is stirred, it will dissipate. When it dissipates, life is lost. Those who cultivate the Tao must not let the life force dissipate. They must contain it within so that they can realize the Tao. This vapor is the energy that creates life. Therefore it is called the precious substance.

Many teachers of Ch'an do not understand the meaning of wisdom and life. They think that by sitting still like death, they will attain the Tao. They do not know that if original nature and life are not united, polishing the mirror will not accomplish anything. Without the techniques of harmonizing and gathering the vapor, the true seed cannot be conceived.

When movement is at rest, the yang force will not be excited and the life energy will not stir. When movement ceases, you should draw the light inward and stop all thoughts and action. This state is called ch'an, or stillness. If you collect the substance at the appropriate time, you will be able to gather the true seed. Draw the substance into the Central Palace and apply the method of closing and opening. Closing and opening refer to internal and external breathing. When inhalation and exhalation are in synchrony, the primordial gate will open and the true seed can enter the path of the jen and tu meridians. Because the breath is used to chase the seed through these channels, this technique is called the Method of the Primordial Movement of the Dharmic Wheel.

The seed is hidden in the lower tan-t'ien. When it circulates, it will return to the original cavity of life. All this is accomplished by turning the Dharmic Wheel. The Child of the Buddha is produced when original nature and life are refined. Wind is used to fan the circulation and draw the light inward. The inward gaze must be sustained for seven days. The mind and the eyes should be directed to the Child so that the three are intertwined. The womb inside is red but the light emanating outside is white. When the tan-t'ien becomes warm, sweet nectar will collect in the mouth. The intention must be still when the Child emerges from the furnace. After the Child is conceived, the fetus and intention must be circulated together. Use softness to subdue hardness and collect that which is flowing with movement. In the cultivation of life, there is no other method than this.

Do not use the "forward" or "backward" methods. The "forward method" refers to techniques of massage and breath control. The "backward method" refers to techniques of concentrated [insight] meditation. These methods do not cultivate original nature and life simultaneously.

There are three openings along the spine. On the left and right of each opening are three cavities that are aligned on top of each other. The Child of the Buddha is tempered in the area below the navel. Once the Child is mature, it must leave its magical environment. If it does not leave, it will have been conceived in vain. When you apply heat to incubate the area below the heart and above the kidneys, you will be enveloped by a bundle of the great harmonious vapor of the celestial realm. You will be in a state of bliss and feel as if you are intoxicated. The Buddha called it the three flavors of ch'an stillness. The Taoists called it the sweet dew that hangs suspended in the middle of space.

Many people do not know that cooperation between the human and the celestial ways is necessary to attain the Tao. The celestial circulation must be guided by intention before it can enter the Central Palace. When the primordial and mundane vapors are at rest, something will emerge from the tan-t'ien. Glowing brightly and suspended in the middle of space, this thing is shapeless and formless. After two or three cycles of inhalation and exhalation, something else will emerge in the tan-t'ien. Formless and glowing, it is the same substance that appeared earlier. At this time, you must use the secret method of the celestial order to gather the light into the womb. Empty your thoughts and cease all actions. Be absolutely still but remain alert. Two streams of the yang substance will then rise from the Bubbling Spring cavity to the top of the head and fall into the Central Palace. When there is no breath coming from the nostrils, the six meridians are at rest. When there is no coming out and going in, you have attained the true reality. Do not let the fetus come out too quickly. When the fetus emerges from the top of the head, it will hover a foot or two above the body. The methods of ch'an kept secret over hundreds of years have now been completely revealed.

THE NINE STEPS OF REFINING THE MIND

*Chiu-tseng
lien-hsin*

THE FIRST STEP in refining the mind is to tame the impure mind. The impure mind is filled with thoughts and idle chatter. Thoughts come from desire, and idle chatter is born from ignorance. When you first practice meditation, you should set aside desire and sever your attachment to the world. Stop the wandering thoughts and the idle chatter. Use the method of observing stillness to dissolve everything into nothingness. Focus on the area behind the navel and in front of the Life Gate. Below it, inside, there is an empty circle. This is where you should direct your inward gaze. Illuminate the mind and suspend it in the sky. Gather it with energy and keep it within the limits. Let the coming and going hover within the square in the circle. Let every breath return to the root to be united with the natural act of creation. You must be firm and still or the mysterious work within will not be clear and clean. The ray of internal light must be connected to the true breath and stay in a state of nondifferentiation and stillness. This is the preliminary work of refining the mind and cultivating the vapor.

The second step in refining the mind is to cultivate the mind of stillness. If the ray of internal light is united with the true energy, it will penetrate the primal darkness and emerge through the mysterious opening. If the mind is unstable, the knowledge-spirit will lead it astray. If mind and vapor are separated, we will not be able to see our original face. The important thing here is not to let knowledge and sense drift when the mind and the breath are in union. Keep the mind within the energy but do not attend to it. Let the energy embrace the mind but do not think about it. In chaos and nondifferentiation, let them become one. This is the work of refining the mind to unite it with energy.

The third step in refining the mind is to cultivate the mind to return it to its proper place. In the previous stage, you have experienced the all-embracing undifferentiated oneness. When yin sinks to its lowest point, the first ray of yang returns. This phenomenon is called the emergence of the mind of the sky and the earth in the One Mysterious Cavity. At this time, generative [ching], vital [ch'i], and spiritual [shen] energy are in the state of pre-creation. In the primal beginning, the three energies are not differentiated, and if the mind is still, this primal energy can be gathered and circulated. When the energy is gathered, you will see things you have never seen and hear sounds you have never heard. But if the mind is not still, everything will fail and the energy will fall into the realm of post-creation. The undifferentiated vapor will be separated into mundane generative, vital, and spiritual energy. The important thing here is that when the Mysterious Gate [or One cavity] first appears, you must step onto the cloud of fire immediately and chase the vapor to the Tail Bone cavity. Calm the mind, soften the breath, hit the iron drum, penetrate the three gates, and let the vapor rest at K'un-lun. This is the work of refining the mind and chasing the vapor.

The fourth step in refining the mind is to cultivate the hidden mind. In the previous stage, you have stepped onto the cloud of fire, penetrated the three gates, and directed the mind and vapor to enter the Mud Ball cavity. However, if the knowledge-spirit is active in the Mud Ball cavity, the vapor will chill and it will not be transformed into the true water. As a result, all the work accomplished in the Three Palaces will come to nothing. The important thing here is to know what should happen on the top of K'un-lun. Use the mind to direct the breath upward so that stillness can be united with the vapor. When the vapor becomes sweet nectar, it will flow from the palate of the mouth down the tongue into the throat. Running down the Descending Tower, it will enter the Yellow Palace and empty into the Primal Ocean. Roaring like thunder, it will sink to the bottom of the sea to wait for the Mysterious Gate to appear again. This is the work of refining the mind to attain the vapor.

The fifth step in refining the mind is to cultivate the mind of good foundation. In the previous stage, the vapor has entered the Mud Ball cavity, the life force has returned to the vapor's cavity, and the waterwheel has been initiated. From now on, you should have only one concern—and this is, do not let the circulation get idle. The foundation is built in one hundred days. If thoughts and desire arise, the foundation of the elixir will not be stable. Building the foundation requires gathering generative energy and uniting it with the spirit. If you do not work hard, generative energy and spirit will dissipate and you will not be able to lengthen your life and attain the Tao. The important thing here is to initiate the circulation in the hours of tzu (11:00 P.M. to 1:00 A.M.) and wu (11:00 A.M. to 1:00 P.M.). Replenish the fuel daily. Use k'an to fill li. Store the generative energy and make the belly firm. This is the work of refining the mind and binding the breath.

The sixth step in refining the mind is to cultivate

its realized nature. In the previous stage, the movement of the waterwheel has been initiated, the generative energy has been collected, and the spirit has
been gathered. The root of the spirit is now steady
and firm. From here on, the nectar of the heart will
descend when the breath of the kidneys rises. This is
the interaction of k'an and li. In the undifferentiated
chaos, you will hear the sound of waves rushing and
roaring. One half of it is the breath of water; the
other half is the breath of mist. This is the first stir-
ring of metal and water. If the mind strays when it is
time to cultivate the jade nectar and circulate the
elixir, all previous efforts will be wasted. The important thing here is that metal and water must separate
when they first emerge from the tan-t'ien. Their
pathways must diverge before they flow to the Bubbling Spring cavity. When they are gathered at the
Tail Bone cavity, true breathing will stop. When the
breath is at rest, you must initiate movement immediately and let the energy flow up to the Celestial
Valley cavity. Then you must swallow the vapor
down the throat and let it sink into the Yellow [Cen-
tral] Palace. If you nourish and moisten it constantly, the mind will be cool and clear. The blood
will become thick, and intention will be gathered
into the earth. Inside earth, mercury, which is the
bright circle of the mind, is born. When the mind is

round and clear, the spirit sword will be secure in your hand and you will be able to cut your attachments to the world. Mencius described this as penetrating the mind and knowing original nature. The Taoist immortals described this as cultivating the yin elixir and the internal pill. This is the work of refining the bright and original nature of the mind.

The seventh step in refining the mind is to cultivate the brightness of original nature. In the previous stage, you have tempered the metal, gathered the water, and initiated the waterwheel. These processes are all part of the internal refinement. Now you must work on external refinement and the union of the external and the internal. When the true mind is centered, it will not stray. However, although the internal body is bright, the mercuric substance can still escape, and although the internal refinement is complete, the yin elixir can still be ruined. If the purity of the vapor is not preserved, original nature may be lost. The important thing here is to put the clear and empty mind, the wondrous principles, and the right amounts of cinnabar and earth in the other's home. Let the other's home be empty and let yours be full. Let there be nothing in the other's home and let the substance be in yours. Use substance to attract nothingness and direct the substance into the void. When the mind is still as death, the primordial vapor of pre-creation will suddenly emerge from the void. In the first cycle, it appears as first yang and is like thunder [the trigram chen]. In the second cycle, it becomes second yang and is like lake [the trigram tui]. In the middle of this cycle you should start to harmonize the elixir. From one side, a waft of true vapor is exhaled, like a tiger emerging from the water. From the other side, a point of mysterious light descends, like a dragon rising from the fire. When the dragon and tiger copulate and original nature and feeling are united, a battle will occur. The sky and the earth will darken and body and mind will be still. The third yang now stirs, its structure resembling the trigram ch'ien [sky, father]. Like water and fire, mist and smoke, frost and snow, and falling flowers, it glows and shines. When this happens, you should immediately grasp the sword in one hand, make the sign of the sword mudra in the other, and walk the steps of the Bushel [Big Dipper]. Shake the primal harmony, increase the heat, let the vapor penetrate the three gates, and guide it to the Mud Ball cavity. All the pores on your skin should now be completely open. This process is different from the movement of the jade nectar in the water-wheel in the previous stage. It is important that you swallow the substance immediately, let pre-creation take control, and unite it with post-creation original nature and life. This process is called the Great Return of the Elixir. Its nature is fire and its number is seven. Life is associated with the element metal. The numeric of metal is nine, and when the nine returns to its origin, the "circulation of the seven and the return of the nine" is complete. From here on, lead will control mercury and the mind will always be bright and firm. This is the work of refining the mind to attain the spirit.

The eighth step in refining the mind is to cultivate the tamed mind and unite it with the spirit. In the previous stage, the seven has returned, the nine has been circulated, and the mind has attained perfect stillness when mercury has been subdued by lead. However, steaming and incubation are still required to transform the vapor into the spirit. The spirit resides in the body, but now and then it must travel outside. In the twelve months of the year, the months mao [fourth month] and yu [tenth month] are used for bathing, and the remaining ten months are dedicated to regulating the flow and the ebb of energy. This process is called the ten months of incubation. If you mistake this to mean ten months in chronological time, the mind will not become numinous even if you have attained absolute stillness. If you refine and temper the mind, the spirit-mind will emerge. When the spirit moves, transformations will occur and the spirit will emerge from the body. At this time you must remain absolutely still and not be distracted by feelings of attachment. This is the work of refining the mind to penetrate the spirit.

The ninth step in refining the mind is to cultivate the mind already joined with the spirit and let it return to the void. In the previous stage, the spirit has emerged from the womb and is in a state of stillness. Now it should follow the movement of intention and travel without obstruction. Let it float with the clouds, wander to far-off places, or let it stay in a state of bliss. If the spirit-mind is not empty, however, it cannot embrace the ten thousand things. This is why the void needs to be cultivated. In cultivating the void, the heart should be empty and completely open. In clarity and stillness, the mind knows intuitively that it is at one with the sky and the earth. It knows that self is not self and emptiness is not empty. The world may be defiled but emptiness is untainted. The universe may be incomplete but emptiness is complete. The spirit fills the void and the Law of the Dharma embraces the illusory world. This is the culmination of the process of refining the mind.

Printed in the United Kingdom
by Lightning Source UK Ltd.
9704200001B/25